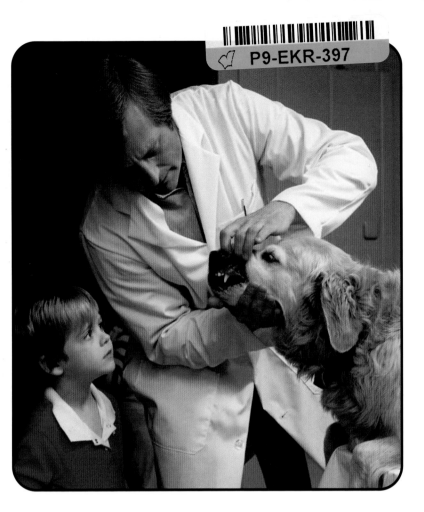

We try to keep our pets healthy.

We give them the care they need.

I give my turtle clean
water each day.

My hamster gets
exercise on his wheel.

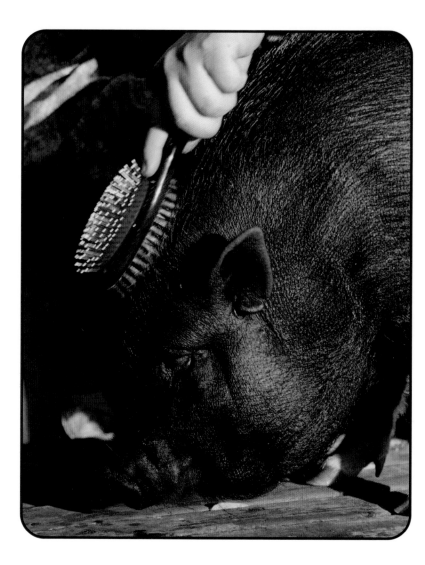

I brush my pig to keep him clean.

We give our goat good food.

I make sure my cat has a
warm place to sleep.

We pet our bunny to make it happy.

It makes us feel happy, too.

My pup needs a lot of love.

I think all pets do.